Chickens

by Robin Nelson

first step nonfiction

Lerner Publications · Minneapolis

What lives on a farm?

Chickens live on a farm.

A female chicken is a **hen**.

A male chicken is a **rooster**.

Chickens have feathers
and wings.

But they cannot fly very far.

Chickens have a **beak**.

They eat seeds and bugs
with their beak.

Hens lay eggs.

Hens sit on the eggs to keep them warm.

The farmer takes some
eggs to eat.

Some eggs are left to **hatch**.

A baby chicken hatches
from an egg.

A baby chicken is called a **chick**.

Chickens give us eggs to eat.

It is fun to see chickens on
the farm!

eye

beak

comb

wattle

wing

tail feathers

feet

Parts of a Chicken

Chickens can be many different colors—brown, black, orange, and white. Chickens have a comb on top of their heads and a wattle below their beak.

How can you tell the difference between a hen and a rooster? Roosters are bigger than hens. Roosters have longer tail feathers too.

Chicken Facts

 Hens lay about 300 eggs a year.

 It takes 21 days for an egg to hatch.

 A chick has a special egg tooth on its beak. The chick uses its egg tooth to help it hatch.

 Chicks chirp a lot so their mother can find them.

Roosters crow loudly.
Hens cannot crow.

 Chickens live in a special
house called a chicken
coop. The coop keeps
them safe at night.

 There are more chickens in
the world than people.

 Eggs can be several different
colors—white, brown, blue,
green, or pink.

Glossary

 beak – a bird's mouth

 chick – a baby chicken

 hatch – break open

 hen – a female chicken

 rooster – a male chicken